Going to the

GREAT SMOKY MOUNTAINS

National Park

FARCOUNTRY
PRESS

HELENA, MONTANA

by Charles W. Maynard

For Caroline, Anna, Jamie, and Chris,
and of course, Anastasia and Ainsley

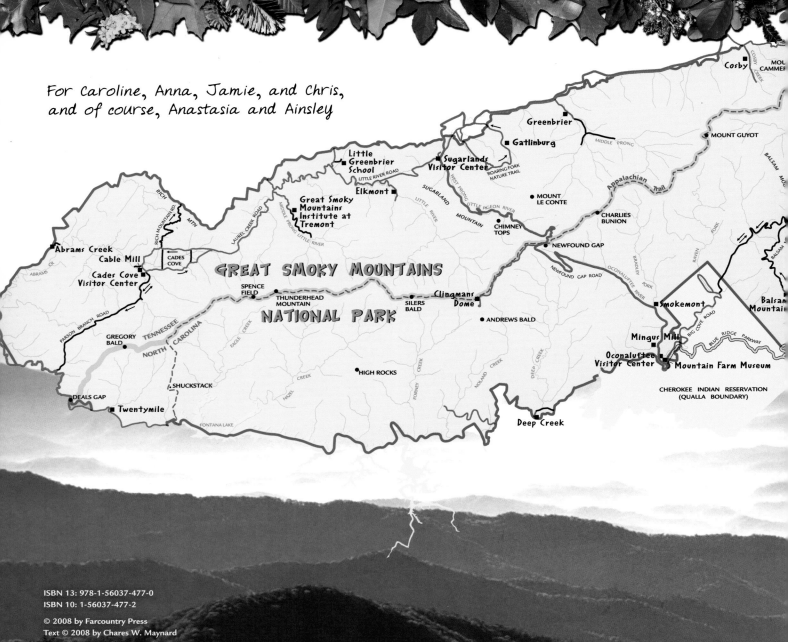

ISBN 13: 978-1-56037-477-0
ISBN 10: 1-56037-477-2

© 2008 by Farcountry Press
Text © 2008 by Chares W. Maynard

Cover and back cover photos (background): Ann and Rob Simpson
Cover photo (bear): ©2008 JupiterImages Corporation
Cover and back cover illustrations: Robert Rath

For more information on our books, write Farcountry Press, P.O. Box 5630,
Helena, MT 59604; call (800) 821-3874; or visit www.farcountrypress.com.

Library of Congress Cataloging-in-Publication Data

Maynard, Charles W. (Charles William), 1955-
  Going to the Great Smoky Mountains National Park / by Charles W. Maynard.
    p. cm.
  ISBN-13: 978-1-56037-477-0 (pbk.)
  ISBN-10: 1-56037-477-2 (pbk.)
  1. Natural history--Great Smoky Mountains National Park (N.C. and Tenn.)--Juvenile literature.
  2. Great Smoky Mountains National Park (N.C. and Tenn.) I. Title.
  QH105.N8M39 2008
  508.768'89--dc22

                 2007031008

Created, produced, and designed in the United States.
Printed in China.

12 11 10 09 08 07   1 2 3 4 5 6

TABLE OF CONTENTS

YOU'RE INVITED

to explore Great Smoky Mountains National Park

WHEN? All year long

WHERE? The Great Smoky Mountains on the border of North Carolina and Tennessee

WHAT TO BRING? Camera, hiking boots, Junior Ranger materials, and this book

No RSVP necessary

Welcome to Great Smoky Mountains National Park! This book will introduce you to a wonderful place full of life and history. You will see wildflowers bordering the trails, playful waterfalls tumbling from mountainsides, elk and deer grazing in the meadows, and mottled salamanders hiding in the creeks. Visit grassy balds where the Cherokee people hunted. Sit in the small houses where mountain farmers raised their families. Explore vast forests thick with trees.

Your adventure in the Smokies begins right here!

> Hey Guys! Welcome to Great Smoky Mountains National Park!

Cades Cove

The Range of Life

Great Smoky Mountains National Park, which was established in 1934, is a lovely, mountainous park, perched on the border between the states of North Carolina and Tennessee. This beautiful park entertains more visitors than any other national park.

Here you can see acres upon acres of tall trees, flowering shrubs, rushing streams, blooming plants, and wild animals. This abundance of life ranges from dainty trilliums to mighty oaks, from bright red salamanders to long-nosed black bears.

The Great Smoky Mountains, also known as a "range of life," may be home to the largest variety of plants and animals of any national park in the United States. Some of these, such as Rugels ragwort and Jordan's red-cheeked salamander, can only be found in the Smokies.

Jordan's red-cheeked salamander

Catesby's trillium

Rugels ragwort

AMAZING

The United Nations selected the Great Smoky Mountains as a World Heritage Site and International Biosphere Reserve because of the park's 2,000 plant and animal species—such as the world's greatest variety of salamanders.

Black bear

THE PLACE OF BLUE SMOKE

Over the years, the Great Smoky Mountains have had many names. The Cherokee Indians once described the mountains *Shaconage*, meaning "Blue, Like Smoke" or "Blue Mists." To the people who lived in the valleys, the large mountains looked blue on the horizon, and, after summer rainstorms, the wisps of clouds that rose from the forest resembled smoke. Later, settlers called the mountains "stone" or "iron" because they were so difficult to travel across. They also called them the "Smoky Mountains" because of the wispy clouds and blue haze that clung to the high peaks.

From a Range of Life to a National Park

Although the idea of forming a national park in these mountains began in the 1890s, Great Smoky Mountains National Park was actually established in 1934 on land donated by the states of Tennessee and North Carolina. When President Franklin Delano Roosevelt dedicated the park six years later, he declared:

There are trees here that stood before our forefathers ever came to this continent; there are brooks that still run as clear as on the day the first pioneer cupped his hand and drank from them. In this Park, we shall conserve these trees, the pine, the redbud, the dogwood, the azalea, the rhododendron, the trout and the thrush for the happiness of the American people.

In its first year, Great Smoky Mountains National Park became the most visited national park in the country. It still is one of the nation's most popular parks, with as many as eight to ten million visitors a year—which is about the population of New York City!

President Franklin Delano Roosevelt

RAIN, TREES, BIRDS & BEES:

Great Smoky Mountains National Park in Numbers

Park Size: 521,000 acres or 800 square miles

Elevations: 840 feet to 6,643 feet

Annual Precipitation: 55 inches in the low areas to 85 inches on the highest peaks

Dogwood

Flame azalea

Flora:
130 tree species
1,600 flowering plants
100 shrub species

Fauna:
more than 240 bird species
66 mammal species
43 amphibian species
39 reptilian species
60 fish species

Trails: more than 800 miles of trails

Waterways: 2,100 miles of streams

Cave salamander

CREATION OF THE SMOKIES

The Cherokee have lived in and around the Great Smoky Mountains for over 1,000 years. According to the Cherokee, the story of the Great Smokies began long ago, when all creatures lived on top of the dome of the sky.

When these animals began looking for a new home, they peered through the holes in the sky through which the stars shine and saw a watery world below. Grandfather Dove flew out to seek land but came back, exhausted, without sighting anything. Grandfather Eagle flew out next, but he, too, returned, without word of land. Grandfather Buzzard then spread his huge wings to glide on the winds, but he didn't have any more success.

Finally, Grandmother Spider said, "Never send a man to do a woman's job!" She flitted over the surface of the water, but she, too, was unable to find land. Undeterred, she dove to the bottom of the endless ocean and brought up some mud and spread it out. She continued this task until she formed all the land.

"It's muddy!" cried all the other animals. Grandfather Buzzard said, "I'll dry it out." He began to flap his huge wings to dry the ground. There was a great deal of muddy earth, and as Grandfather Buzzard grew tired, he began to fly lower and lower.

When he flew close to the ground, his mighty wings struck the mud and dug deep valleys. When he raised his wings, mountains were formed. The animals all shouted, "Stop! You will ruin everything!" But it was too late. Buzzard had already formed the Great Smoky Mountains. The Cherokee called the mountains, "The Land Where the Buzzard Tired."

The Geological Story of the Smokies' Creation: A Tale in Two Parts

Build 'Em Up

The Great Smoky Mountains are a small portion of the Appalachian Mountains, which are some of the world's oldest mountains. The story of the creation of these mountains is dramatic and happens in two parts.

First is a story about rocks. The Great Smokies' rocks were once part of mountains more than a billion years old, which were eroded into soil, silt, sand, and gravel. These deposits were then pressed into a layer of rock nearly 9 miles thick. Most of the rocks in the Smokies were formed approximately 800 to 545 million years ago; the oldest lie on the park's North Carolina side, the youngest in Cades Cove, Tennessee.

Next is a story about **tectonic plates,** or blocks of earth's crust. Somewhere between 310 and 245 million years ago, tectonic plates in the North American and African continents bumped together and formed a supercontinent! Over millions of years, this force lifted the entire Appalachian mountain chain from Newfoundland, Canada, to Alabama and "cooked" the sedimentary rocks into harder, metamorphic rocks. These mountains may once have been as tall as today's Rocky Mountains.

tectonic plates

Appalachian Mountains

tectonic plates

Wear 'Em Down

As soon as the mountains were uplifted, ice, rain, and wind started to wear them down. Geologists say the mountains are eroding at the rate of about 2 inches every thousand years. Although glaciers did not come as far south as the Smokies during the Ice Age, extreme cold and constant freezing and thawing caused the mountains to erode faster. Water has shaped the Smokies into a land of steep-sided valleys and mile-high-plus peaks.

SHAKE & BAKE

During the heat and pressure of continental collision, rocks changed type or metamorphosed into different rocks. Sandstone turned into quartzite. Shale became slate. Granite became gneiss.

The metamorphic backbone of the Chimney Tops is visible through the lush vegetation.

WHAT A VIEW!

Clingmans Dome Observation Tower

On Top of Old Smoky

Drive up Newfound Gap Road (U.S. Highway 441), the road that slices the Great Smoky Mountains in half, to get a sweeping view of the park. A spur road (closed in winter) takes you to Clingmans Dome. Walk to the observation tower, where you will be rewarded with cool air and breathtaking mountain views, including Mount Le Conte, Silers Bald, and distant Thunderhead Mountain.

HOW BIG IS BIG?

Clingmans Dome	6,643 feet
Mount Guyot	6,621 feet
Mount Le Conte	6,593 feet
Mount Buckley	6,580 feet
Mount Love	6,420 feet

What's in a Name?

In southern Appalachian terms, a **"gap"** is a low point in a mountain ridge, something New Englanders call "notches" and westerners call "passes." Indian Gap was a low point where the Cherokee and other native people followed a game trail through the mountains. Later, surveyors found a lower gap for a road, which became known as "New Found" or Newfound Gap.

A **bald** is a peak covered with grass or shrubs and very few trees. The Cherokee hunted on balds, because the grass attracted deer, elk, and bison. Andrews and Gregory balds are grassy balds, where farmers used to graze their livestock. Other balds, such as Maddron Bald between Gatlinburg and Cosby, are covered with shrubs, such as rhododendron or mountain laurel, and are called "laurel slicks" or "laurel hells" by mountain people.

Mountain laurel

Mountain people called the mountain valleys **"coves."** Coves are wide valleys where, in later years, people often farmed because the soil was rich, not as rocky, and level. Cades Cove, in Great Smoky Mountains National Park, and Tuckaleechee Cove and Wears Cove, outside the park, are good examples of this feature.

Indian Gap

Waterways

The Smokies get a lot of moisture. Annual precipitation averages 55 inches in the valleys to 85 inches or more on the highest peaks. Over the years, this moisture has shaped the landscape: Streams have cut through upraised rock, creating V-shaped valleys. The creeks and rivers act as conveyor belts, slowly moving the rocks and soil of the mountains into the valleys and river deltas downstream.

Water pouring over steep slopes also creates waterfalls. Laurel Falls, Ramsey Cascades, Rainbow Falls, and Abrams Falls are some of the most popular waterfalls—and hiking destinations—in the park. Grotto Falls is fun to visit because the Trillium Gap Trail passes behind the falls!

Meigs Falls near Little River

LIVING ON OLD SMOKY

This atlatl point was found in the park and is estimated to be 9,000 years old.

The first humans came to the Great Smoky Mountains at least 11,000 years ago. They settled in the rich river bottoms, traveling up into the surrounding mountains in search of deer, elk, bison, and other wild game. They also crossed the mountains through gaps to hunt in the valleys, such as Cades Cove and Cataloochee.

The Principle People

Although many native people lived around the Smokies, the Cherokee dominated the area from the 1500s until the late 1700s. Related linguistically to the Iroquois, "the Principle People," as the Cherokee called Indians, lived along the fertile river flats. Their name for themselves was *Ani-Kituhwa* or "People of Kituhwa." They hunted in the mountains and cleared trees from some mountaintops so the grassy areas would attract game.

Each Cherokee village had a seven-sided council house representing the seven clans of the Cherokee: Bird, Paint, Deer, Wolf, Blue, Long Hair, and Wild Potato. Each clan selected two chiefs: one for peace and one for war. The tribe was a matriarchy, which means it traced its descendents through its women, and women had an equal voice in tribal affairs.

Cherokee warrior in front of seven-sided council house

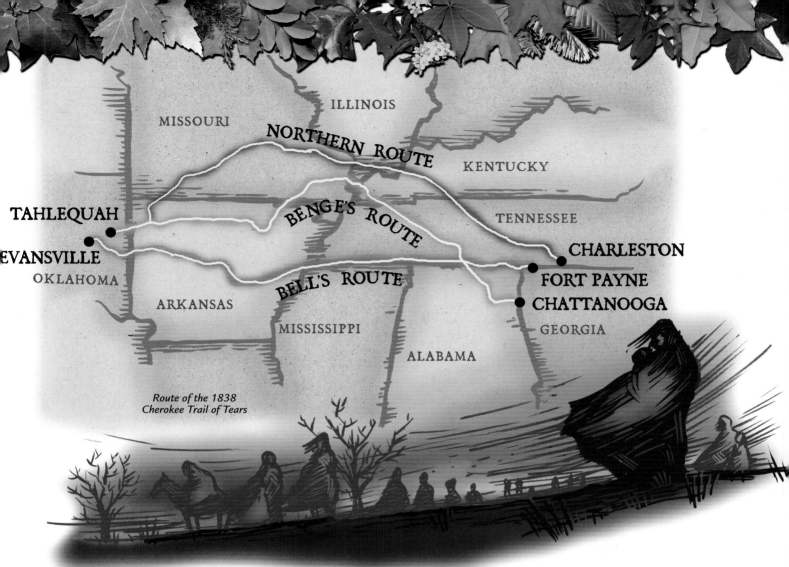

Route of the 1838
Cherokee Trail of Tears

The Trail Where They Cried

Life changed dramatically for the Cherokee when European settlers arrived in the mountain valleys in the late 1700s. When the settlers moved into the mountains, the Cherokee were pushed from their traditional lands, and conflicts between the two groups erupted. When gold was discovered on Cherokee lands, the U.S. Congress ratified the Treaty of New Echota on May 23, 1836, which forced the Cherokee to move.

Beginning in October 1838, Cherokee men, women, and children were forced to walk 1,000 miles for six months from the Great Smoky Mountains to Indian Territory (now Oklahoma). During this tragic event known as the "Trail of Tears," more than 4,000 of the 16,000 Cherokee who made the long, difficult journey died of cold, starvation, and hunger. The Cherokee term for the trail is *Nunna dual Tsuny*, or "Trail Where They Cried."

During this time, several groups of Cherokee fought and won the right to stay on land they owned, others hid in the Smoky Mountains and were later allowed to stay. Still others returned to the area after the Trail of Tears. Their descendents, the 11,000-member Eastern Band of the Cherokee, currently live on the Qualla Boundary around Cherokee, North Carolina. Some of them speak the Cherokee language and practice the traditional ways. You can learn about their fascinating history at museums in Cherokee, North Carolina.

TRAIL OF TEARS

"Long time we travel on way to new land. People feel bad when they leave Old Nation. Womens cry and make sad wails. Children cry and many men cry...but they say nothing and just put heads down and keep on go towards West. Many days pass and people die very much."

—Recollections of a
Trail of Tears survivor,
Trail of Tears National Park Site

SEQUOYAH

Sequoyah, a Cherokee Indian born in 1770, developed an alphabet of 86 characters for the Cherokee language. This alphabet was adopted by the Cherokee and used widely throughout the Cherokee Nation by the early 1820s. The Cherokee Council even established a newspaper, the ***Cherokee Phoenix,*** and ordered a printing press with type for the Cherokee alphabet.

A Sample of the Cherokee Alphabet

Ꭰ a
Ꭶ ga Ꭷ ka
Ꭽ ha
Ꮃ la
Ꮉ ma
Ꮎ na Ꮏ hna Ꮐ nah
Ꮖ qua
Ꮜ sa Ꮝ s
Ꮧ da Ꮤ ta
Ꮬ dla Ꮭ tla
Ꮳ tsa
Ꮹ wa
Ꮮ le
Ꮇ me
Ꮑ ne
Ꮗ que
Ꮞ se
Ꮥ de Ꮦ te
Ꮯ tle
Ꮴ tse
Ꮺ we
Ᏸ ye
Ꭲ i
Ꭹ gi

The Non-Native People; Spanish and English Explorers

Hernando de Soto

The Spanish, led by explorers Hernando de Soto in 1540 and Juan Pardo in 1567, were the first Europeans to see the Smokies and the surrounding valleys. One of Pardo's men called the area around the Smokies, "The Land of Angels." The Spanish searched for gold and other minerals, but instead found fertile valleys with native people farming and hunting along the rivers and in the mountains.

About 100 years later, the first English traders entered the area. The natives who lived around the mountains traded animal hides for metal objects such as knives, hoe blades, and mirrors and swapped other goods with the Europeans who lived near the coast in South Carolina and Georgia. These traders mapped the area and used the rivers in the same way we use highways today—as an easy way to cross the mountains.

Corn Cakes and Venison: Early Settlers

The white settlers scraped out a simple life in the late 1700s. In the mountains, they cleared fields of stone and trees to plant crops of corn and wheat. They cultivated apples in orchards on the steep slopes and hunted wildlife for meat. Later mountain people built water-powered mills on the streams to grind corn into meal for cornbread, corn mush, spoon bread, or corn cakes.

A typical log home for a family was approximately the size of our present-day family room, a mere 18 feet by 20 feet, which would house a family of two parents, 5 to 12 brothers and sisters, and maybe even grandparents. During the snowy winter days, families were often house-bound, and cabin fever set in. People amused themselves by playing games such as "I Spy" or mumblety-peg, strumming banjos or singing ballads, crafting toys such as whimmy diddles or cornhusk dolls, quilting, and telling hunting stories or Jack tales.

The Davis–Queen House

Mountain children gather outside their log home in 1886

A WINTER'S MEAL

In the summer, food was eaten fresh from the garden. In winter, fare was limited to food that could be stored, dried, pickled, or salted. Choices included: cornbread, dried beans, pickled vegetables, cornbread, potatoes, mush, dried or sulfured apples, cornbread, salted pork, chicken, cornbread, stack cake, molasses, and, yes, more cornbread!

SONGS OF THE SMOKIES

"ON TOP OF OLD SMOKY"

On top of Old Smoky
All covered with snow,
I lost my true lover
For courting too slow.

Now courting is pleasure
And parting is grief,
And a false-hearted lover
Is worse than a thief.

The lyrical strains of the well-known song—which every schoolchild has sung in its original and spaghetti-themed version—underlines a plaintive story of lost love. Light-hearted, "fun" songs like this were popular, such as **"Down in the Valley."** Story songs, which told stories of murders or desertions, such as **"Barbara Allen"** or **"The Drunkard's Last Drink,"** were also popular.

Popular hymns, such as **"Amazing Grace"** or **"The Old Rugged Cross,"** reflect the more spiritual side of life in the Smokies. Many hymnals used a shape note notation to display the tunes. Seven shapes were used to indicate the pitch of each note.

Shape notes

Mountain musicians

Historic sawmill

This subsistence lifestyle came to an end in the early 1900s with the arrival of logging. Logging boom towns, such as Proctor, Smokemont, Tremont, and Elkmont, grew up quickly around sawmills. In a short time, instead of growing and hunting their own food, people began cutting down logs, selling them, and buying store-bought food. Over the next 30 years, large tracts of virgin forest were cut down and hauled away. Loggers cleared whole mountainsides until not a tree remained. Ridges eroded and filled the streams with mud and silt.

You can explore the houses of families who lived in the Smokies by visiting Cades Cove, Cataloochee, and Roaring Fork. The Great Smoky Mountains National Park has the largest collection of historic log buildings in the National Park System. Seven churches from old communities still stand, as do two schoolhouses, and several grist mills.

Cataloochee

In 1814, the Cataloochee Valley was settled by the Caldwell family, followed by the Hannahs, Bennetts, Nolands, Palmers, and Woodys. Today houses, barns, churches, and schools are evidence of the once-thriving community that farmed and raised apple orchards here. See the elegant, 1906 Caldwell House, the rugged Hannah Cabin, and Palmer's Chapel, where after a death a bell would toll out the age of the deceased.

The headstones in the cemeteries remind us of the hardships endured by the residents of the Smokies. Because of the lack of medical care, many infants and children died of diseases such as measles and the flu.

Gravestones at Cataloochee

Cades Cove

The Cherokee called Cades Cove *Tsiyahi,* meaning "Otter Place," long before it was first settled by John and Lucretia Oliver in 1817. By 1850, a settlement of 132 houses filled the mountain cove. Farmers cultivated the fields and grazed their livestock in the high mountain meadows. See how the settlers lived in the 1800s by taking the one-way, 11-mile road through Cades Cove to visit the historic cabins, a grist mill, a variety of barns, and three churches. You can see a miller grind corn into meal at Cable Mill or watch a quilting demonstration in the Becky Cable House.

QUILTS

Mountain people wasted nothing. Cloth scraps from old clothes were stitched together into quilts. Mountain women arranged the scraps into patterns that commemorated events or told stories. The Double Wedding Ring pattern, for example, often celebrated an anniversary. The Log Cabin pattern symbolized hearth and home. Friendship quilts had the stitched signatures of friends and family, while a Crazy quilt was pieced together with no pattern at all.

Walker sisters inside their home

Walker sisters sitting on the front porch of their home in Little Greenbrier

The Walker Sisters

The five Walker sisters lived in the house built by their father and mother, John and Margaret Walker, in Little Greenbrier in the mid-1840s. In the traditional Appalachian way, the five women, along with four brothers and two other sisters, grew up on their parents' small farm. The family grew their own food, spun their own yarn, and wove cloth for their clothing.

Five of the Walker daughters who never married—Hettie, Margaret Jane, Polly, Louisa Susan, and Martha Ann—continued to live in the house long after their parents died. Although the Great Smoky Mountains National Park was created in 1934, the Walkers did not finally deed their house to the park until 1941, on the condition that they could continue living there until their deaths. The last sister, Louisa Susan, died in 1964 at the age of 82. You can walk through the log house, corn crib, and springhouse to get an idea of what life was like in a mountain cabin.

To take the 2.2-mile hike, go to the parking area of the 1882 Little Greenbrier Schoolhouse, half a mile above Metcalf Bottoms Picnic Area. To reach Metcalf Bottoms, drive 9.5 miles from the Sugarlands Visitor Center and 8.5 miles from the Townsend "Y" on Little River Road.

MY MOUNTAIN HOME

There is an old weather bettion house
That stands near a wood
With an orchard near by it
For all most one hundred
years it has stood

It was my home in infancy
It sheltered me in youth
When I tell you I love it
I tell you the truth

by Louisa Susan Walker

THE BIRTH OF A NATIONAL PARK

In the early 1900s, many people wanted to create a national park in the southern Appalachian Mountains to protect the area. In 1872, Congress created its first national park in Yellowstone, and in 1916, the National Park Service was formed.

532:-RAINBOW FALLS GREAT SMOKY MOUNTAINS NATIONAL PARK

President Calvin Coolidge signed a bill in 1926 to authorize a national park in the Great Smoky Mountains. North Carolina and Tennessee worked together to buy land from lumber companies and farmers. Individuals also contributed money, including schoolchildren who gave pennies, nickels, and dimes to save the Smokies.

President Calvin Coolidge

One of the richest men in the country, John D. Rockefeller, Jr., added $5 million to the fund in memory of his mother, Laura Spellman Rockefeller.

But creating a park in the Great Smoky Mountains was not simple. Many landowners held deeds to Smokies' land. Land had to be dickered over, and the people who lived there had to leave their homes. Some were glad to leave, but others were angry. Some were allowed to stay for a short time, but because they could not hunt, trap, or cut timber, they could not practice their traditional lifestyles.

BEAUTIFUL VIEW OF MT. LE CONTE—16

GREAT SMOKY MOUNTAINS NATIONAL PARK, TENN.—N. C.

Old postcards of Great Smoky Mountains National Park

PRESIDENT ROOSEVELT SPEAKING AT THE DEDICATION OF THE GREAT SMOKY MOUNTAINS NATIONAL PARK.

N-414

LAURA SPELMAN ROCKEFELLER MEMORIAL. "PHOTO BY TENN. STATE DEPT. OF CONSERVATION"

Rockefeller Memorial

President Franklin D. Roosevelt signed the bill establishing Great Smoky Mountains National Park in 1934. When he dedicated the park on September 2, 1940, he stood at Newfound Gap with his left foot in North Carolina and his right foot in Tennessee. In his speech, he said:

The old frontier, that put the hard fibre in the American spirit and the long muscles on the American back, lives and will live in these untamed mountains to give to the future generations a sense of the land from which their forefathers hewed their homes.

Today you can visit the Rockefeller Memorial and stand with a foot in both states, just the way President Roosevelt did.

The CCC

From 1933 to 1942, young men from all over the country worked in the Civilian Conservation Corps (CCC), which was also called "Roosevelt's Tree Army." In the Smokies, the CCC built many of the park's trails, roads, campgrounds, and elegant stone bridges. They also built fire lookouts, including the very unusual Mount Cammerer Lookout, where a fire watcher lived in a two-story stone-and-timber tower at 5,025 feet on the state line between North Carolina and Tennessee. At an old CCC campsite in Cades Cove, the corps' handiwork reappears each spring. Daffodils planted by the young men spell "CO 5427," which was their company's number.

Mount Cammerer Lookout

Kephart Prong Trail leads to an old CCC campsite

"This is one of the best lives a man could live. Right here. Peace and quiet. The day I left that tower it was beautiful... It was heaven is what it was."

—Lenny Garver, former National Park Service employee at Mount Cammerer in the Smokies

PLANT LIFE IN THE SMOKIES

From White Oaks to Fraser Firs:

Trees in the Smokies

Because of the mountains' height and the area's range of elevations, the Smokies are home to more tree species than almost anywhere in the world. The park hosts 130 tree species, more than in all of Europe, 100 of which are native tree species. By contrast, Yellowstone National Park, which is five times the size of Great Smoky Mountains National Park, has only nine tree species.

When the canopy of hardwood leaves turns various hues of red, yellow, orange, and brown in autumn, the scenery is varied and beautiful. Carloads of visitors crowd the roadways of the Smokies to see this annual fall display. The "tree-peeping" season lasts from early October through mid-November.

Nearly 20 percent of the park is **old-growth forest,** which means that the trees were never harvested. Some trees can be more than 100 feet tall and 350 years old. Seek out an old-growth forest to get a glimpse of the past: This is what most of the Smokies originally looked like! Albright Grove is one of the best areas of old-growth forest. You can also find some pockets of old-growth forest in the Cataloochee Valley and just beyond Laurel Falls on the Cove Mountain Trail.

200-LOOP NEAR NEWFOUND GAP GREAT SMOKY MOUNTAINS NATIONAL PARK

Old-growth forest near Chimneys

Tulip trees

Forest Types

As you drive from Cherokee to the crest of the Smokies, the change in climate and vegetation is similar to the difference you would experience driving from Tennessee to Canada. As you travel uphill on Highway 441 (Newfound Gap Road), you can look for five major forest types.

Enormous tulip poplar trees tower over open forest floors, and eastern hemlocks, Carolina silverbells, and Fraser magnolias grow to enormous sizes. When one of these ancient giants is knocked over during a summer storm, it tears a hole in the green canopy and allows light to reach the forest floor, which encourages new growth. More than 80 percent of the park is covered in deciduous forest, which means the trees drop their leaves every year. Imagine how different the woods look in winter and spring!

Tulip tree flower

6,000 feet

5,000 feet

4,000 feet

3,000 feet

2,000 feet

1,000 feet

Spruce-fir forests crown the highest peaks of the Smokies, such as Mount Le Conte and Clingmans Dome, starting at elevations from 4,500 to 6,000 feet. The main tree species are the red spruce and Fraser fir. A non-native insect, the balsam woolly adelgid, has killed nearly 90 percent of the Fraser firs.

How big? **Fraser fir:** 80 feet tall, 30 inches around

Northern hardwood forests are in the high mountains at elevations from 3,500 to 5,000 feet, where the climate is cooler and moist. Tree species include beech, birch, striped maples, white basswood, and yellow buckeye. When temperatures drop, the leaves turn bright colors of red, yellow, and orange, similar to forests in New England, New York, and Pennsylvania.

How big? **American beech:** 90 feet tall, 3 feet around

Pine-oak forests exist on the dry, exposed ridge tops on the park's western edge at elevations from 1,000 to 4,500 feet. Common trees are pines (including pitch, table mountain, and white), and oaks (black, chestnut, red, and scarlet). Hickories can also be found.

How big? **Scarlet oak:** 80 feet tall, 3 feet around

Hemlock forests are at elevations of 1,000 to 3,000 feet in moist areas and 4,000 feet in drier areas. Called the "redwoods of the East," great stands of hemlocks cover hundreds of acres throughout the park. These giant trees are being killed by the non-native hemlock woolly adelgid.

How big? **Eastern hemlock:** 100 feet tall, 4 feet around

Cove hardwood forests are located from 1,000 to 3,500 feet. They include the greatest variety of tree species, including basswoods, beeches, buckeyes, Carolina silverbells, eastern hemlocks, Fraser magnolias, hickories, yellow birches, yellow buckeyes, and tulip poplars.

How big? **Tulip poplar:** 100 feet tall, 4 feet around

Checklist of Common Wildflowers

EARLY SPRING
- [ ] bloodroot
- [ ] spring beauty

SPRING
- [ ] galax
- [ ] Jack-in-the-pulpit
- [ ] lady's slipper orchid
- [ ] Solomon's seal
- [ ] trillium (10 different species)

SUMMER
- [ ] cardinal flower
- [ ] crimson bee-balm
- [ ] spiderwort

EARLY FALL
- [ ] ironweed
- [ ] Joe-pye-weed

Lady's slipper orchid

From Trilliums to Asters: Wildflower National Park

Imagine visiting a place where, from early spring to late fall, you can see flowers ranging from snowy white trilliums to yellow lady's slipper orchids, from brilliant red cardinal flowers to wild-leaved sunflowers! That place is Great Smoky Mountains National Park, home of more than 1,600 species of flowering plants, also known as "Wildflower National Park."

Many visitors flock to the Smokies each April for the spring wildflower pilgrimage. This five-day festival features hikes and programs and has introduced people to the beauty of mountain flowers for more than 50 years.

Ironweed

DO NOT PICK THE FLOWERS!

Spiderwort

Jack-in-the-pulpit

Red trillium

Wildflowers in Cades Cove

Mountains Afire

From March through August, the Smokies' nearly 110 native shrub species, ranging from flame azaleas to Catawba rhododendrons, put on a colorful display. One native shrub, the flame azalea, lives up to its name with beautiful red, orange, and yellow flowers that "blaze" in the high mountains. William Bartram, a botanist in the 1700s, said flame azaleas were "the most gay and brilliant flowering shrub yet known" and made the mountains look as if they were on fire.

The closely related mountain laurel and rhododendron bloom in pink and white profusion from early May in the lower elevations to August on the high peaks. When Catawba rhododendrons, which live at elevations over 3,500 feet, are in blossom in June, whole mountaintops turn pink.

There are beautiful nonflowering plants in the park, including ferns, club mosses, horsetails, and bryophtes, such as liverworts and hornworts.

Catawba rhododendrons

Horsetails   *Hornworts*

Flame azalea

Bloodroot flower   *Bloodroot*

WILDFLOWER DYE

The Cherokee used the dark reddish-brown juice from the roots of white bloodroots to paint themselves or to dye cloth and baskets. Early settlers used a drop of the root juice as cough medicine. The Cherokee also brewed tea from yellow lady's slipper orchids roots—also called whippoorwill shoes or Noah's arks—to help with flu, colds or nerves.

Yellow patches amanita

Fly agaric

Caesar's amanita

Viscid violet cort

Yellow powder amanita

Fungi, Toadstools, and Lichens— Oh My!

In the Smokies, there are thousands of species of **fungi** (the plural of the word fungus), or organisms that often live off other plants. You may see fungi on trees, dead logs, or growing in the shade. Some fungi are called mushrooms or toadstools, but there are many different shapes and colors ranging from bright orange to purple. Fungi can look like a toadstool, as well as a small shelf, a piece of coral, or even a brain.

Lichens grow on rocks and trees and are interesting mixes of algae and fungus. The lichen's green part is algae, which makes food for the fungus part of the plant, which attaches the plant to the rock or tree. This little ditty is a good way to remember lichens: "Freddy Fungus met Allie Algae and took a lichen to her."

Lichen

BEWARE OF POISON MUSHROOMS

WILDLIFE OF THE SMOKIES

From mammals to fish, amphibians to reptiles, and birds to insects, wildlife is abundant in the Great Smoky Mountains National Park. Many people see the park's larger mammals, such as deer and bear, but the watchful explorer will see many more. Look closely among the ferns on the forest floor for salamanders. Listen in the shrubs and treetops for the hundreds of birds that populate the park. Stand in the dark to see the tiny lights of amazing fireflies.

Checklist of Common Mammals

- [ ] black bear
- [ ] coyote
- [ ] Eastern gray squirrel
- [ ] elk
- [ ] raccoon
- [ ] red fox
- [ ] red squirrel
- [ ] river otter
- [ ] white-tailed deer
- [ ] wild boar

Black Bear

The black bear is *the* animal most people think of when they think of the Great Smoky Mountains. Although black bears once lived in most of North America, they were rarely seen in the park when park land was established in 1934. Now their population in the park is the densest in the world—the park has an average range of 1,200 to 2,000 bears.

Fed Bears are Dead Bears!

Peanut butter sandwiches, watermelons, apple cores, and fried chicken are deadly for bears. When bears eat these foods, they lose their fear of humans and can become aggressive toward people. Protect the bears by disposing of your garbage in bear-proof containers or taking it with you.

BEAR FACTS

- Bears are 60 to 72 inches in length and can stand 30 to 37 inches at the shoulders.

- Bears live from 12 to 15 years.

- Bears are **omnivores,** which means they live on berries, nuts, other plants, and animals. They can double their weight by fall as they prepare for the long winter.

- Bears can run approximately 30 miles per hour.

DO NOT FEED THE ANIMALS!

Black bear

ELK FACTS

- Adult elk measure 7 to 10 feet long and are 5 feet tall at the shoulders. Bulls (males) have antlers that span 5 feet, which they shed each year.

- Elk live approximately 15 years. A newborn calf weighs 35 pounds and can stand in the first minutes of its life.

- Elk are **herbivores,** which means they eat plant materials, such as bark, leaves, acorns, and buds, as well as grasses.

DEER FACTS

- Adult deer measure 5 to 7½ feet long, and are 3 to 3½ feet tall at the shoulders. Bucks (males) have antlers that span 3 to 4 feet, which they shed each year.

- Deer live approximately 10 years. A newborn fawn weighs about 3 to 6 pounds and can walk at birth.

- Deer are **herbivores,** which means that they eat plant materials, such as bark, leaves, acorns, and buds, as well as grasses.

Elk

Elk

The largest animal in the park and the largest animal in the deer family, elk once grazed throughout the Smokies. By the early 1800s, however, elk numbers dwindled because of overhunting and loss of habitat.

In 2001, the National Park Service experimented with reintroducing 25 elk to the Cataloochee Valley. The effort succeeded. By 2007, the herd had grown to 80 and it continues to thrive.

The best time to view elk is in the early morning or at dusk in the meadows and forests. Cloudy, rainy days are also good for spotting elk. If you see an elk, stay at least 200 feet away—that's about the size of a hockey rink. Stay on the trail and watch them with binoculars.

White-tailed Deer

With their wide eyes, black noses, and long legs, deer are a familiar sight in Great Smoky Mountains National Park. Although they are usually seen in open meadows in Cataloochee Valley and Cades Cove, nearly 6,000 deer live throughout the Smokies!

In late June, the delicate fawns are born. The pattern of white spots on their coats protects them from predators. The spots **camouflage** or hide fawns from their predators. Bears, bobcats, and coyotes prey on the young and the ill, which keeps the deer population in check.

White-tailed deer

Song Dogs in the Smokies

Coyotes were first seen in the Great Smoky Mountains in 1982, and today on quiet evenings, you might hear the sound of the song dogs' distinctive yips in the distance. Coyotes have established themselves as major predators in every area of the park. Looking like medium-size dogs, coyotes measure from 44 to 53 inches. They live from 10 to 14 years and can run fast—nearly 40 miles an hour! Coyotes' diets vary, from berries to birds, from garbage to grass, from melons to moles, and from snakes to snails.

Gray squirrel

Squirrels: From Fliers to Boomers

The Great Smoky Mountains have five types of squirrels: fox, red, southern flying, northern flying, and gray squirrels. The uncommon fox squirrel is the largest at 3 pounds. The red squirrel is smaller, and is found at higher elevations. The smallest and most acrobatic are the flying squirrels, although they are not commonly seen in the Smokies. These squirrels don't really fly— they glide through the air on a flap of skin that extends from their front paws to their back legs like a sail.

Red squirrel

River Otter

River otters began disappearing because of over-hunting in the 1920s. In 1986, the National Park Service successfully reintroduced the northern river otter to the park. Playful animals with black noses, long whiskers, and webbed feet, they are excellent swimmers and divers. Otters build dens under logs, in riverbanks, in natural hollows, and in the abandoned burrows of other animals. They often hunt at night in rivers and creeks, such as the Little River, Cataloochee Creek, and the Oconaluftee River.

Flying squirrel

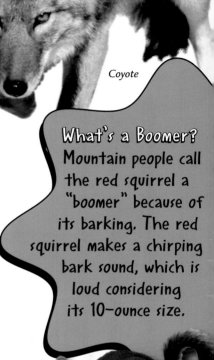

Coyote

What's a Boomer?
Mountain people call the red squirrel a "boomer" because of its barking. The red squirrel makes a chirping bark sound, which is loud considering its 10-ounce size.

Red squirrel

River otter

FACTS YOU OTTER KNOW

- Otters measure from 35 to 50 inches long.
- Otters live 8 to 9 years in the wild.
- Otter pups weighs 5 ounces at birth and are 10 inches long.
- Otters can stay underwater for 8 minutes and can run 18 miles per hour.

Checklist of Common Birds

- [ ] barred owl
- [ ] black-throated blue warbler
- [ ] Carolina chickadee
- [ ] chestnut-sided warbler
- [ ] dark-eyed junco
- [ ] downy woodpecker
- [ ] goldfinch
- [ ] peregrine falcon
- [ ] pileated woodpecker
- [ ] raven
- [ ] ruffed grouse
- [ ] turkey vulture
- [ ] veery
- [ ] winter wren

Turkey Vulture

Birds

From black-capped chickadees to northern saw-whet owls, from blue-headed vireos to rose-breasted grosbeaks, from downy woodpeckers to yellow-rumped warblers: Birds love the Smokies! So do bird-watchers. They have spotted 240 different species, although only about 60 species live in the park all year round. Some birds, such as the magnolia warbler and the Swainson's thrush, stop only long enough to rest and feed on their yearly migration from places as far away as South America and Canada. Others, including the scarlet tanager and the chipping sparrow, stay the summer to build a nest and have young.

Keep your ears open for bird calls! You are more likely to hear the different birds than you are to see them. Listen to their varied songs. The small dark-eyed junco will click and chirp to distract you from its nest. The ruffed grouse will boom away by flapping its wings. At night, owls hoot and whippoorwills trill, letting you know that some birds work best in the dark.

Raven

Barred owl

Goldfinch

Hairy woodpecker

Yellow-rumped warbler

Peregrine Falcon

With its hooked beak, yellow legs, and pointed wings, the peregrine falcon is an amazing bird of prey. It feeds on other birds, diving at speeds of nearly 200 miles per hour and capturing them in midair! Peregrine falcons used to live in the Smokies, but from the 1940s until the 1970s, falcons and other birds of prey came close to extinction because of insect pesticides such as DDT. Falcons did not return to the Smokies until the mid-1990s, when they began nesting and having young near Peregrine Peak on Little Duckhawk Ridge ("duck hawk" is a name mountain people used for falcon). They can now be seen along the flanks of Mount Le Conte, in Greenbrier, and in the Cataloochee Valley.

Peregrine falcon

From Bass to Brookies

Brook trout

Bass, darters, lamprey, minnows, suckers, and trout—the Smokies have 60 different species of fish in its clear mountain brooks and creeks. Yet even though the park boasts nearly 2,100 miles of streams, fish live in only 800 miles of its waterways. Why?

Brook trout, or brookies as they are known, are the only trout native to the Smokies. Once found throughout the area, the fish lost much of their habitat because of logging and the introduction of non-native rainbow trout. Today, brook trout are once again living in about 133 miles of the park's streams. Rainbow and brown trout live in large streams in the park's lower elevations.

Little River

Home Sweet Home

Please remember you are a visitor in what is a home to many animals.

Be respectful. Stay far away from wild animals and give them plenty of space. Carry binoculars so you can view wildlife from far away.

The park rule: Willfully approaching bear or elk within 50 yards (150 feet), or any distance that disturbs or displaces them, is prohibited.

Throw away all of your garbage. Do not leave food, even crumbs, for the creatures—there is plenty of food for them in the forest.

WHAT'S IN A NAME?

Many mountain people called creeks or streams "forks" and "prongs." Look for these interesting names on signs and maps: Bradley Fork, Raven Fork, and Middle Prong.

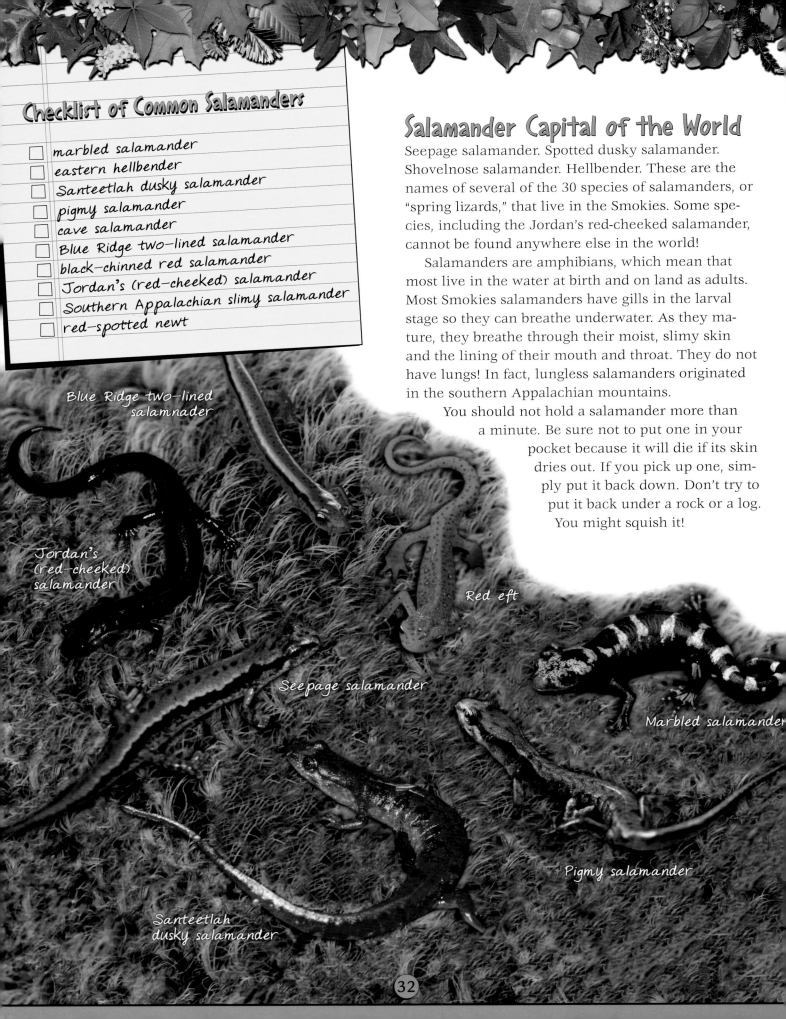

Checklist of Common Salamanders

- [ ] marbled salamander
- [ ] eastern hellbender
- [ ] Santeetlah dusky salamander
- [ ] pigmy salamander
- [ ] cave salamander
- [ ] Blue Ridge two-lined salamander
- [ ] black-chinned red salamander
- [ ] Jordan's (red-cheeked) salamander
- [ ] Southern Appalachian slimy salamander
- [ ] red-spotted newt

Salamander Capital of the World

Seepage salamander. Spotted dusky salamander. Shovelnose salamander. Hellbender. These are the names of several of the 30 species of salamanders, or "spring lizards," that live in the Smokies. Some species, including the Jordan's red-cheeked salamander, cannot be found anywhere else in the world!

Salamanders are amphibians, which mean that most live in the water at birth and on land as adults. Most Smokies salamanders have gills in the larval stage so they can breathe underwater. As they mature, they breathe through their moist, slimy skin and the lining of their mouth and throat. They do not have lungs! In fact, lungless salamanders originated in the southern Appalachian mountains.

You should not hold a salamander more than a minute. Be sure not to put one in your pocket because it will die if its skin dries out. If you pick up one, simply put it back down. Don't try to put it back under a rock or a log. You might squish it!

Blue Ridge two-lined salamnader

Jordan's (red-cheeked) salamander

Red eft

Seepage salamander

Marbled salamander

Santeetlah dusky salamander

Pigmy salamander

Timing is Everything

As the sun goes down on the long summer evenings in the Smokies, small lights begin to light up the sky. They are fireflies—14 species of fireflies, to be exact! These fireflies or lightning bugs are beetles that cast a greenish-yellow light (although one species has a distinctive bluish light).

Each species has a unique flash pattern that helps males and females recognize each other. In Elkmont in mid-June, you can see amazing fireflies, known as **synchronous fireflies,** flashing their lights at the same time! Many people come to watch this special show—it's the only place it happens in the United States.

Fireflies produce light by combining the chemical *luciferin* and *oxygen* with the enzyme *luciferase* in their abdomens—or lanterns. This is one form of *bioluminescence.* Can you say that backward?

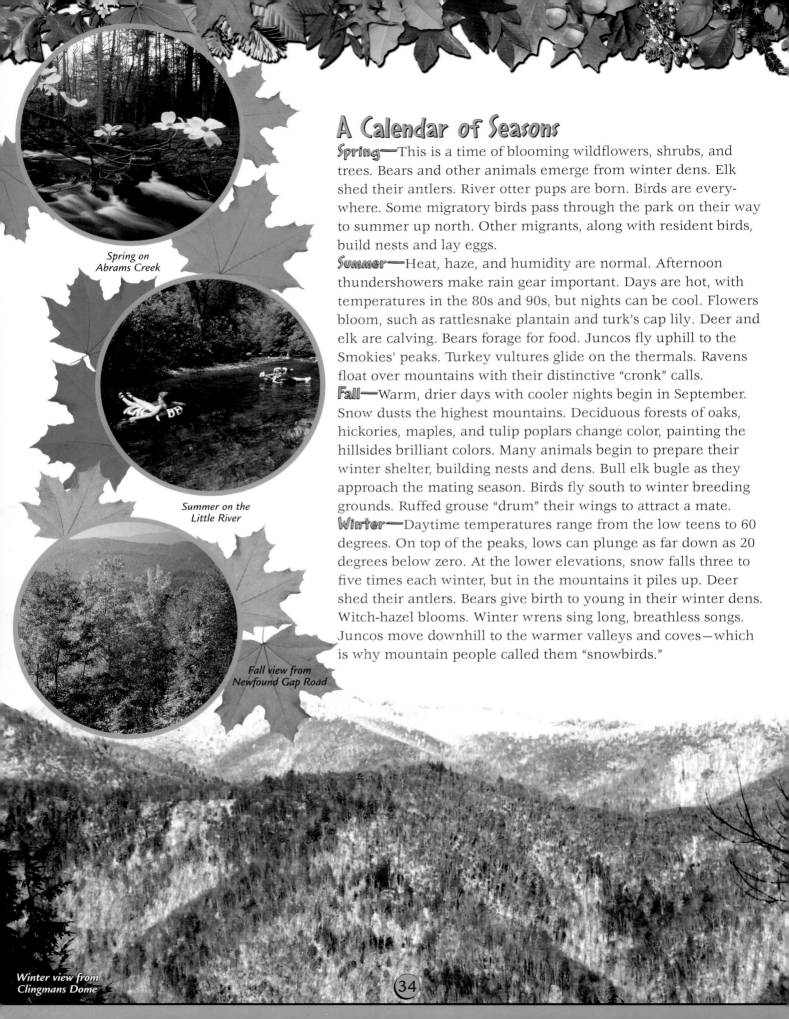

Spring on
Abrams Creek

Summer on the
Little River

Fall view from
Newfound Gap Road

Winter view from
Clingmans Dome

A Calendar of Seasons

Spring—This is a time of blooming wildflowers, shrubs, and trees. Bears and other animals emerge from winter dens. Elk shed their antlers. River otter pups are born. Birds are everywhere. Some migratory birds pass through the park on their way to summer up north. Other migrants, along with resident birds, build nests and lay eggs.

Summer—Heat, haze, and humidity are normal. Afternoon thundershowers make rain gear important. Days are hot, with temperatures in the 80s and 90s, but nights can be cool. Flowers bloom, such as rattlesnake plantain and turk's cap lily. Deer and elk are calving. Bears forage for food. Juncos fly uphill to the Smokies' peaks. Turkey vultures glide on the thermals. Ravens float over mountains with their distinctive "cronk" calls.

Fall—Warm, drier days with cooler nights begin in September. Snow dusts the highest mountains. Deciduous forests of oaks, hickories, maples, and tulip poplars change color, painting the hillsides brilliant colors. Many animals begin to prepare their winter shelter, building nests and dens. Bull elk bugle as they approach the mating season. Birds fly south to winter breeding grounds. Ruffed grouse "drum" their wings to attract a mate.

Winter—Daytime temperatures range from the low teens to 60 degrees. On top of the peaks, lows can plunge as far down as 20 degrees below zero. At the lower elevations, snow falls three to five times each winter, but in the mountains it piles up. Deer shed their antlers. Bears give birth to young in their winter dens. Witch-hazel blooms. Winter wrens sing long, breathless songs. Juncos move downhill to the warmer valleys and coves—which is why mountain people called them "snowbirds."

Boars, Bugs & Bad Air: Aliens in the Park

A number of "alien" species from other places are causing trouble in the park. Descendants of European boars or wild hogs that were brought to a North Carolina hunting reserve in 1912 wandered into the Smokies in the late 1940s and have been making a mess ever since. The boars now live in the park, rooting for food at night, turning the soil upside down, and opening up areas for bird-borne foreign seeds.

Two other aliens are insects that threaten entire forests: balsam woolly adelgids and hemlock woolly adelgids. The balsam woolly adelgid has killed most of the mature Fraser fir trees in the park's higher elevations, such as along the Newfound Gap and Clingmans Dome roads. The hemlock woolly adelgid is attacking the abundant eastern hemlocks, which can live up to 600 years. The National Park Service is working to save old-growth hemlocks and those in popular areas by using insecticides and by releasing tiny beetles the size of poppy seeds that feed on the insects.

Another major "alien" in the park is air pollution. Air pollution is carried by wind currents from nearby cities—from power plants, industries, and automobiles—to the Smokies. Two types of pollution are damaging the Smokies: sulphur and ozone pollution. Sulphur from coal-fired power plants and other sources combines with water to produce acid rain. The clouds above the park's peaks not only obscure views, they can be more acidic than vinegar!

Nitrogen oxides from power plants, car fumes, and other sources break down in the sunlight to become ground-level ozone, a poisonous form of oxygen. Ozone levels in the Smokies can become dangerous, worsening lung problems in adults and children and injuring plants, such as black cherry trees, milkweed, and sassafras.

European hog

Hemlock woolly adelgids

GOTCHA!

Spraying to control hemlock woolly adelgids

Luna moth

Brown-spiketail dragonfly

Northern pearly eye butterfly

Snail

Discovering Life

Imagine trying to discover every single form of life in the Great Smoky Mountains! Well, beginning in 1997, scientists have been trying to count every living organism in Great Smoky Mountains National Park in a project called the All Taxa Biodiversity Inventory (ATBI).

Scientists think there may be 100,000 species in the park, but believe that only about 12,000 have been identified to date. As of 2006, volunteer scientists, students, and citizens had discovered more than 4,666 forms of beetles, dragonflies, moths, mushrooms, snails, and other organisms that no one knew existed in the Smokies. Keep on top of this cutting-edge research—and be the first one on your block to hear of the world's newest plants, mushrooms, or bugs by visiting www.discoverlifeinamerica.org.

Visitors study the waters from the bridge by the Caldwell House

One fish, two fish...

TAKE A HIKE

One of the best ways to experience the park is to get out of the car and walk. You can see wildlife, waterfalls, scenic views, historic cabins, and wildflowers along the park's 150 trails. There are more than 800 miles of hiking trails in the park. Here is a sampler of hikes to help you enjoy the Smokies, up close and personal.

Caldwell House

Woody House

CATALOOCHEE AREA

Round-trip: 2 miles (3.2 kilometers)
Time: 1½ to 2 hours
Difficulty: easy to moderate
Trailhead: Begin this walk at the upper end of the Cataloochee Valley. From Interstate 40 in North Carolina, take Exit 20 and turn onto Cove Creek Road. Follow the winding road 11 miles into the Cataloochee Valley.

Palmer House

Cataloochee

1 mi
1.6 km

WOODY HOUSE TRAIL

Palmer's Chapel

The trail follows an old roadbed along Rough Fork to the Woody House, crossing the stream three times on foot logs. Constructed of logs in the late 1800s, the Woody House was enlarged as the family grew. The house and springhouse are all that remain of the once-sprawling farm. Keep your eyes open for wildlife in this beautiful valley named *Gadalutsi* by the Cherokee, which means "wave upon wave." Don't miss the Cataloochee Valley's Palmer Chapel, Beech Grove School, the Palmer House and Museum, and the Caldwell House.

Woody House

A thirsty hiker takes a welcome rest

Laurel Falls and Big Trees

GATLINBURG AREA

Round-trip: 4.5 miles (7.24 kilometers)

Time: 3½ hours

Difficulty: moderate

Trailhead: From Sugarlands Visitor Center, drive 3.5 miles toward Cades Cove on Little River Road to Fighting Creek Gap. Come early on weekdays or weekend mornings: the parking area fills up quickly.

Because of its mountain views, the falls, and the old-growth trees, the Laurel Falls Trail is one of the Smokies' most popular spots. The paved trail winds through mountain laurel to Laurel Falls, an 80-foot-high, two-tiered falls along Laurel Branch. Cross Laurel Branch on the walkway between the upper and lower falls and continue on the half-mile dirt trail to a grove of 150-foot, old-growth tulip poplar trees.

LAUREL FALLS AND BIG TREES TRAIL

2.25 mi
3.62 km

Laurel Falls

To Cades Cove

Fighting Creek Gap

Little River Road

Laurel Falls Trail

Great Smoky Mountains hikers

Hemlock trees

Grotto Falls

GATLINBURG AREA

Round-trip: 3 miles (4.8 kilometers)

Time: 2 hours

Difficulty: moderate

Trailhead: The trail begins in a parking area at stop 5 of the Roaring Fork Motor Nature Trail, 2 miles from the beginning of the one-way road (closed in winter). To reach the Motor Nature Trail from downtown Gatlinburg, drive 3.7 miles up Cherokee Orchard Road. Arrive early—the parking area fills up quickly.

GROTTO FALLS TRAIL

Roaring Fork Motor Nature Trail

one-way

1.5 mi
2.4 km

Grotto Falls

Trillium Gap Trail

The Trillium Gap Trail passes behind the scenic 25-foot-high Grotto Falls! Enjoy old-growth hemlock trees, salamanders in Roaring Fork, and pileated woodpeckers. The 5-mile, one-way Roaring Fork Motor Nature Trail features several old homesites and a mill.

Clingmans Dome

GATLINBURG/CHEROKEE AREA

Round-trip: 1 mile (1.6 kilometers)
Time: 1 hour
Difficulty: steep
Trailhead: The Forney Ridge parking area off Clingmans Dome Road 7 miles from Highway 441 at Newfound Gap. To reach Clingmans Dome Road (closed November to April), take Highway 441 20 miles north from Cherokee and 15 miles south from Gatlinburg.

CLINGMANS DOME TRAIL

For 360-degree views of the Smokies, take the paved trail from the parking area, then climb the Clingmans Dome tower for views of mountains and valleys 25 miles away. The tower straddles the border between Tennessee and North Carolina and rises directly above the Appalachian Trail. The elevation of this short walk is more than a mile above sea level—watch how a bag of chips or a water bottle inflates as the altitude increases from the surrounding lowlands.

Clingmans Dome Trail

OCONALUFTEE RIVER TRAIL

Oconaluftee River Trail

CHEROKEE AREA

Round-trip: 3 miles (4.8 kilometers)
Time: 1½ to 2 hours
Difficulty: easy
Trailhead: Begin at the Oconaluftee Visitor Center near Cherokee, North Carolina.

The Oconaluftee River Trail leads from the visitor center and Mountain Farm Museum to the town of Cherokee. Interpretive signs, in English and Cherokee, reflect on the spiritual and cultural meaning of the Great Smoky Mountains to the Cherokee Indians

Oconaluftee River Trail

Indian Creek Falls

BRYSON CITY AREA

Round-trip: 2.4 miles (3.9 kilometers)

Difficulty: easy to moderate

Trailhead: Begin at the trailhead at the upper end of the Deep Creek picnic area. To find the picnic area, follow signs through downtown Bryson City, North Carolina.

INDIAN CREEK FALLS TRAIL 2.4 mi 3.9 km

Juney Whank Falls • Indian Creek Falls • Tom Branch Falls ■ Deep Creek Campground

This hike is a fun way to see three great waterfalls: Tom Branch Falls, Indian Creek Falls, and Juney Whank Falls. Deep Creek Trail follows an old roadbed along Deep Creek popular with tubers, where you will pass Tom Branch Falls. At 0.7 mile, turn right onto Indian Creek Trail and walk 100 yards to the 25-foot-high Indian Creek Falls. After 0.10 mile, turn left onto Deep Creek Horse Trail and follow signs to Juney Whank Falls. Many people tube down Deep Creek from Indian Creek to the park boundary.

Indian Creek Falls

Abrams Creek

ABRAMS FALLS TRAIL 2.5 mi 4 km

Abrams Falls

Cades Cove Visitor Center

Abrams Falls

CADES COVE AREA

Round-trip: 5 miles (8 kilometers)

Time: 4 hours

Difficulty: moderate

Trailhead: The trailhead is at the end of Abrams Falls Spur Road, stop number 10 on Cades Cover Loop Road, approximately 5 miles up Cades Cove from the park entrance. Along the way, you will pass the Oliver House and three churches, as well lush fields fringed by mountains.

This popular trek leads to Abrams Falls, a 20-foot-high waterfall that plunges over a small cliff into a lovely pool below named for the Cherokee Chief Abram.

Le Conte Lodge

IN THE GATLINBURG AREA

Alum Cave Trail: 10 miles round-trip (16 kilometers)
Description: Steep uphill, fast downhill.

The Boulevard Trail: 16 miles round-trip (25.7 kilometers)
Description: Rolling terrain with a steep climb to the peak.

Bull Head Trail: 14.4 miles round-trip (23.17 kilometers)
Description: Steep climb to nice overlooks and a heath bald.

Rainbow Falls Trail: 13 miles round-trip (21 kilometers)
Description: Steep climb to waterfalls and overlooks.

Trillium Gap Trail: 13 miles round-trip (21 kilometers)
Description: A strenuous rocky hike along Roaring Fork Creek to Grotto Falls.

Time: Approximately 5½ to 7 hours, depending on route
Note: Reservations required in far advance.

Le Conte Lodge is a collection of log buildings near the summit of 6,593-foot Le Conte. You must hike up one of five approach trails to stay in the old-timey lodge that began operating in 1926—just eight years before Great Smoky Mountains National Park was created. With washbasins, kerosene lamps, and hearty family-style meals, the lodge offers a unique visit into the Great Smoky Mountains backcountry. Open March through November, the lodge begins taking reservations on October 1 for the following season. Llamas, which supply the lodge, can be seen trekking up the Trillium Gap Trail every Monday, Wednesday, and Friday during the season.

Rainbow Falls Trail along Le Conte Creek

Le Conte Lodge

Llamas going to Le Conte Lodge

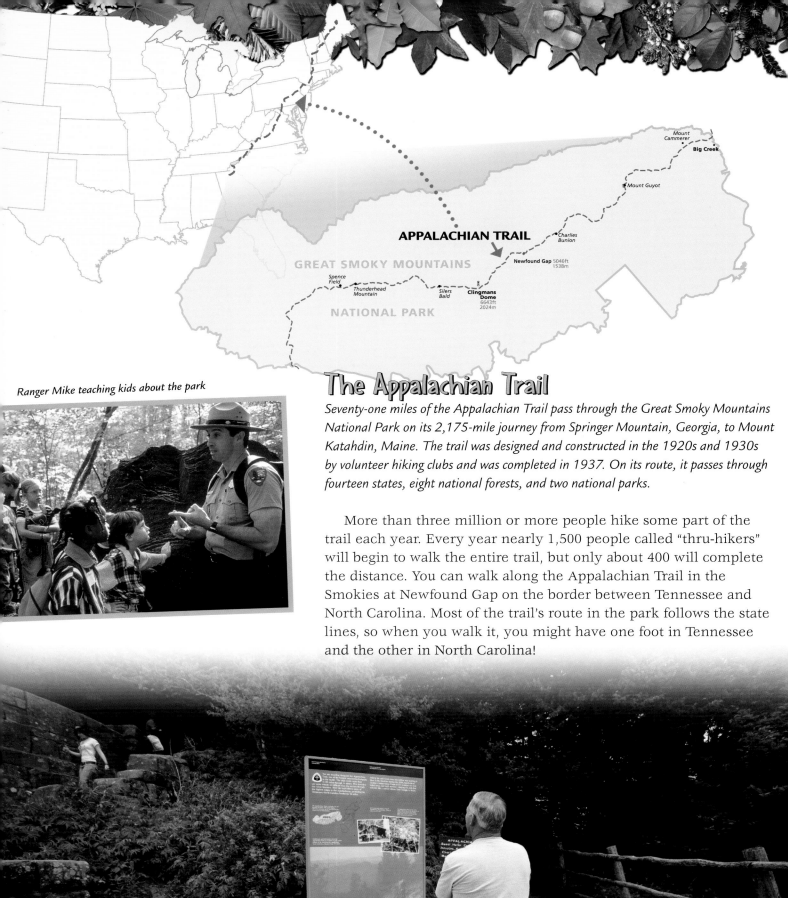

APPALACHIAN TRAIL

GREAT SMOKY MOUNTAINS

NATIONAL PARK

Mount Cammerer
Big Creek
Mount Guyot
Charlies Bunion
Newfound Gap 5046ft 1538m
Spence Field
Thunderhead Mountain
Silers Bald
Clingmans Dome 6643ft 2024m

Ranger Mike teaching kids about the park

The Appalachian Trail

Seventy-one miles of the Appalachian Trail pass through the Great Smoky Mountains National Park on its 2,175-mile journey from Springer Mountain, Georgia, to Mount Katahdin, Maine. The trail was designed and constructed in the 1920s and 1930s by volunteer hiking clubs and was completed in 1937. On its route, it passes through fourteen states, eight national forests, and two national parks.

More than three million or more people hike some part of the trail each year. Every year nearly 1,500 people called "thru-hikers" will begin to walk the entire trail, but only about 400 will complete the distance. You can walk along the Appalachian Trail in the Smokies at Newfound Gap on the border between Tennessee and North Carolina. Most of the trail's route in the park follows the state lines, so when you walk it, you might have one foot in Tennessee and the other in North Carolina!

The Appalachian Trail

A visitor stands at an interpretive sign in Newfound Gap

BIKE, RIDE, CAMP: JUST GET OUT OF THE CAR!

There is no better way to discover the wonders of the Great Smoky Mountains than by getting outside. In the open, you'll experience the park through your senses. Bike through Cades Cove, and you'll drink in the cool, dusty scents of oak trees and see the bright fields of wild-flowers shadowed by the snow-capped Thunderhead Mountain. Listen to the lazy clip-clop of your horse as you ride up the quiet, hemlock-lined trail, along a rushing mountain stream, as squirrels chatter and black-capped chickadees call feee-bee. And what better way to end your day than by cozying up to the campfire, watching fireflies or picking out constellations before you trundle off to your tent?

A family cycling in the Smokies

Cades Cove Cycling

Biking is a wonderful way to experience the park: riding in the shadow of the tall trees, hearing the birds, feeling the cool breezes, and seeing the wildflowers. You can rent bicycles in Cades Cove in summer and fall or bring your own. From early May to late September, the road in Cades Cove is closed to cars on Wednesday and Saturday mornings until 10 A.M. Enjoy pedaling in the lush valley of Cades Cove, past old barns, churches, log homes—and, perhaps, deer. Surrounded by rugged, 5,000-feet peaks, the Cataloochee Valley is also a great spot to bike.

Hi Ho Silver!

Riding a horse is a great way to get into the back-country of Great Smoky Mountains National Park to see enormous trees, abundant wildflowers, and elusive animals like the black bear and the ruffed grouse. Four horse stables offer rides for hourly rates (age and weight restrictions). For information, check with visitor centers, the *Smokies Guide,* or www.nps.gov/grsm/planyourvisit.

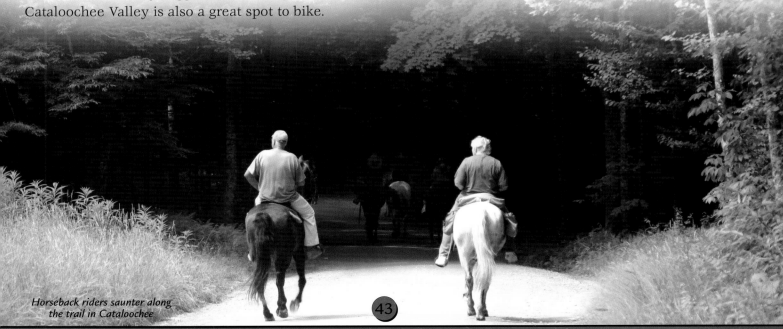

Horseback riders saunter along the trail in Cataloochee

Spend the Night in the Smokies

Sleeping out in a tent, cooking marshmallows over a campfire, breathing in the cool night air: Car camping in the park is a summertime treat. And the Smokies at night are interesting. As the sun sets, deer, elk, owls, and raccoons come out. Fireflies light up the forest. Also, because you are far away from city lights, you can see more stars. Stand outside without a flashlight. Allow your eyes to adjust (it takes the human eye about 30 minutes to get used to the dark), and try to see constellations such as the Summer Triangle, the Big Dipper, and the North Star.

You can bring your own tent and stay in one of the ten campgrounds in the Great Smoky Mountains National Park. Most campgrounds are first-come, first-served and vary in size from 12 sites at Big Creek to 220 sites at Elkmont, and in elevation from 1,125 feet at Abrams Creek to 5,310 feet at Balsam Mountain. The Elkmont, Cades Cove, and Smokemont campgrounds require reservations from May 15 to October 31.

Outdoor Dining

Ten picnic areas offer wonderful places to enjoy a meal outside. Eat your sandwiches at a table shaded by tall trees, beside a rushing stream, or in a green cove. Just make sure you dispose of your garbage in bear-proof trash containers or take it with you.

Camping in the Great Smoky Mountains

BE A JUNIOR RANGER

If you are between the ages of 5 and 12, you can be the proud owner of a Junior Ranger badge by completing the activities in a Junior Ranger booklet. It's easy. Just purchase the booklet at any park visitor center or at the Cades Cove or Elkmont campgrounds. When you have completed the activities in the booklet, return it to a ranger, and the badge is yours!

You can see corn ground into meal, tour a smokehouse, or learn about area plants and animals by visiting the exhibits at one of Great Smoky Mountains National Park's three visitor centers. See Cable Mill, the grist mill where farmers ground corn into meal, at Cades Cove Visitor Center. See cornhusk dolls and quilts as you wander through the Mountain Farm Museum at Oconaluftee near Cherokee. Explore the Smokies' natural history at the Sugarlands Visitor Center. The *Smokies Guide,* the official newspaper of Great Smoky Mountains National Park, offers a list of ranger-led activities, as well as pictures and articles, that will introduce you to the park's wonders.

Cornhusk doll

Children learn about the wonders of the Smoky Mountains through the Parks as Classrooms Program

A future park ranger?

A group of children during a ranger-led activity

Kids learning about the environment
at the Great Smoky Mountains
Institute at Tremont

Researchers at the Appalachian
Highlands Science Learning Center

Science in the Smokies

Environmental education for children and adults happens year-round at the **Great Smoky Mountains Institute at Tremont.** You can learn about the 14 different kinds of fireflies, study bears, build a fire without matches, and learn to eat as the mountain people did. The institute offers day and overnight camps for children, adults, and families on topics ranging from field ecology to photography. For more information, call 865-448-6709 or go to www.GSMIT.org.

The Appalachian Highlands Science Learning Center, one of 17 National Park Service learning centers in the country, offers researchers wonderful opportunities to work on a variety of topics ranging from salamanders to the earth's ozone. For more information, call (828) 926-6251 or go to www.nps.gov/grsm/naturescience/pk-homepage.ngm.

Soundscapes

Some people like to stop at scenic overlooks to see the views—the beautiful sweep of rolling mountains in the Great Smokies—but make sure you also stop to hear the area's unique soundscapes. Stop at one of the park's Quiet Walkways. These short trails are wonderful places away from the roads, where you can hear rushing water, bird song, rustling leaves, and other sounds of the forest. How many different sounds can you hear?

Other Resources on the Smokies

The Great Smoky Mountain Salamander Ball
by Lisa Horstman
(Great Smoky Mountains Association, 1997).

**Scavenger Hike Adventures:
Great Smoky Mountains National Park**
by Kat and John LaFevre
(Le Conte Press, 2004).

The Smokies Yukky Book
by Doris Gove and Lisa Horstman
(Great Smoky Mountains Association, 2006).

Time Well Spent: Family Hiking in the Smokies
by Hal Hubbs, Charles Maynard, and David Morris
(University of Tennessee Press, 2008).

The Troublesome Cub in the Great Smoky Mountains
by Lisa Horstman
(Great Smoky Mountains Association, 2001).

About the author

Charles W. Maynard is an ordained United Methodist minister who works with the Camp and Retreat Ministry of the Holston Conference in east Tennessee and in southwestern Virginia. He has an undergraduate degree from Emory and Henry College and a master of divinity from the Candler School of Theology at Emory University. The first executive director of Friends of Great Smoky Mountains National Park, Charles has written 20 children's books as well as national park guidebooks, including *Time Well Spent,* a family hiking guide to the Great Smoky Mountains National Park that he wrote with Hal Hubbs and David Morris. He and his wife, Janice, have two daughters, Caroline and Anna, and two granddaughters, Anastasia and Ainsley.

Fall view of Newfound Gap

Photo and Illustration Credits

Historic mountain homestead at Oconaluftee